This Address Book Belongs to

Name:
_____

Address:
_____

_____

Phone Number:
_____

E-mail:
_____

Birthdays & Anniversaries

January

_____   _____
_____   _____
_____   _____
_____   _____
_____   _____

February

_____   _____
_____   _____
_____   _____
_____   _____
_____   _____

March

_____   _____
_____   _____
_____   _____
_____   _____

Birthdays & Anniversaries

April

_____   _____
_____   _____
_____   _____
_____   _____
_____   _____

May

_____   _____
_____   _____
_____   _____
_____   _____
_____   _____

June

_____   _____
_____   _____
_____   _____
_____   _____
_____   _____

Birthdays & Anniversaries

July

_____   _____

_____   _____

_____   _____

_____   _____

_____   _____

August

_____   _____

_____   _____

_____   _____

_____   _____

_____   _____

September

_____   _____

_____   _____

_____   _____

_____   _____

_____   _____

Birthdays & Anniversaries

October

_____   _____
_____   _____
_____   _____
_____   _____
_____   _____

November

_____   _____
_____   _____
_____   _____
_____   _____
_____   _____

December

_____   _____
_____   _____
_____   _____
_____   _____
_____   _____

A

Name:	
Address:	
Home:	Cell:
Work:	Fax:
E-mail:	
Birthday:	
Notes:	

Name:	
Address:	
Home:	Cell:
Work:	Fax:
E-mail:	
Birthday:	
Notes:	

Name:	
Address:	
Home:	Cell:
Work:	Fax:
E-mail:	
Birthday:	
Notes:	

A

Name:
Address:
Home: Cell:
Work: Fax:
E-mail:
Birthday:
Notes:

Name:
Address:
Home: Cell:
Work: Fax:
E-mail:
Birthday:
Notes:

Name:
Address:
Home: Cell:
Work: Fax:
E-mail:
Birthday:
Notes:

A

Name:	
Address:	
Home:	Cell:
Work:	Fax:
E-mail:	
Birthday:	
Notes:	

Name:	
Address:	
Home:	Cell:
Work:	Fax:
E-mail:	
Birthday:	
Notes:	

Name:	
Address:	
Home:	Cell:
Work:	Fax:
E-mail:	
Birthday:	
Notes:	

Name:
Address:
Home: Cell:
Work: Fax:
E-mail:
Birthday:
Notes:

Name:
Address:
Home: Cell:
Work: Fax:
E-mail:
Birthday:
Notes:

Name:
Address:
Home: Cell:
Work: Fax:
E-mail:
Birthday:
Notes:

B

Name:

Address:

Home:	Cell:
Work:	Fax:

E-mail:
Birthday:
Notes:

Name:

Address:

Home:	Cell:
Work:	Fax:

E-mail:
Birthday:
Notes:

Name:

Address:

Home:	Cell:
Work:	Fax:

E-mail:
Birthday:
Notes:

B

Name:

Address:

Home:	Cell:
Work:	Fax:

E-mail:
Birthday:
Notes:

Name:

Address:

Home:	Cell:
Work:	Fax:

E-mail:
Birthday:
Notes:

Name:

Address:

Home:	Cell:
Work:	Fax:

E-mail:
Birthday:
Notes:

B

Name:	
Address:	
Home:	Cell:
Work:	Fax:
E-mail:	
Birthday:	
Notes:	

Name:	
Address:	
Home:	Cell:
Work:	Fax:
E-mail:	
Birthday:	
Notes:	

Name:	
Address:	
Home:	Cell:
Work:	Fax:
E-mail:	
Birthday:	
Notes:	

B

Name:	
Address:	
Home:	Cell:
Work:	Fax:
E-mail:	
Birthday:	
Notes:	

Name:	
Address:	
Home:	Cell:
Work:	Fax:
E-mail:	
Birthday:	
Notes:	

Name:	
Address:	
Home:	Cell:
Work:	Fax:
E-mail:	
Birthday:	
Notes:	

C

Name:	
Address:	
Home:	Cell:
Work:	Fax:
E-mail:	
Birthday:	
Notes:	

Name:	
Address:	
Home:	Cell:
Work:	Fax:
E-mail:	
Birthday:	
Notes:	

Name:	
Address:	
Home:	Cell:
Work:	Fax:
E-mail:	
Birthday:	
Notes:	

C

Name:	
Address:	
Home:	Cell:
Work:	Fax:
E-mail:	
Birthday:	
Notes:	

Name:	
Address:	
Home:	Cell:
Work:	Fax:
E-mail:	
Birthday:	
Notes:	

Name:	
Address:	
Home:	Cell:
Work:	Fax:
E-mail:	
Birthday:	
Notes:	

C

Name:	
Address:	
Home:	Cell:
Work:	Fax:
E-mail:	
Birthday:	
Notes:	

Name:	
Address:	
Home:	Cell:
Work:	Fax:
E-mail:	
Birthday:	
Notes:	

Name:	
Address:	
Home:	Cell:
Work:	Fax:
E-mail:	
Birthday:	
Notes:	

C

Name:	
Address:	
Home:	Cell:
Work:	Fax:
E-mail:	
Birthday:	
Notes:	

Name:	
Address:	
Home:	Cell:
Work:	Fax:
E-mail:	
Birthday:	
Notes:	

Name:	
Address:	
Home:	Cell:
Work:	Fax:
E-mail:	
Birthday:	
Notes:	

D

Name:	
Address:	
Home:	Cell:
Work:	Fax:
E-mail:	
Birthday:	
Notes:	

Name:	
Address:	
Home:	Cell:
Work:	Fax:
E-mail:	
Birthday:	
Notes:	

Name:	
Address:	
Home:	Cell:
Work:	Fax:
E-mail:	
Birthday:	
Notes:	

D

Name:
Address:

Home: Cell:
Work: Fax:
E-mail:
Birthday:
Notes:

Name:
Address:

Home: Cell:
Work: Fax:
E-mail:
Birthday:
Notes:

Name:
Address:

Home: Cell:
Work: Fax:
E-mail:
Birthday:
Notes:

D

Name:	
Address:	
Home:	Cell:
Work:	Fax:
E-mail:	
Birthday:	
Notes:	

Name:	
Address:	
Home:	Cell:
Work:	Fax:
E-mail:	
Birthday:	
Notes:	

Name:	
Address:	
Home:	Cell:
Work:	Fax:
E-mail:	
Birthday:	
Notes:	

Name:
Address:

Home: Cell:
Work: Fax:
E-mail:
Birthday:
Notes:

Name:
Address:

Home: Cell:
Work: Fax:
E-mail:
Birthday:
Notes:

Name:
Address:

Home: Cell:
Work: Fax:
E-mail:
Birthday:
Notes:

F

Name:
Address:
Home:	Cell:
Work:	Fax:
E-mail:
Birthday:
Notes:

Name:
Address:
Home:	Cell:
Work:	Fax:
E-mail:
Birthday:
Notes:

Name:
Address:
Home:	Cell:
Work:	Fax:
E-mail:
Birthday:
Notes:

F

Name:	
Address:	
Home:	Cell:
Work:	Fax:
E-mail:	
Birthday:	
Notes:	

Name:	
Address:	
Home:	Cell:
Work:	Fax:
E-mail:	
Birthday:	
Notes:	

Name:	
Address:	
Home:	Cell:
Work:	Fax:
E-mail:	
Birthday:	
Notes:	

F

Name:	
Address:	
Home:	Cell:
Work:	Fax:
E-mail:	
Birthday:	
Notes:	

Name:	
Address:	
Home:	Cell:
Work:	Fax:
E-mail:	
Birthday:	
Notes:	

Name:	
Address:	
Home:	Cell:
Work:	Fax:
E-mail:	
Birthday:	
Notes:	

F

Name:	
Address:	
Home:	Cell:
Work:	Fax:
E-mail:	
Birthday:	
Notes:	

Name:	
Address:	
Home:	Cell:
Work:	Fax:
E-mail:	
Birthday:	
Notes:	

Name:	
Address:	
Home:	Cell:
Work:	Fax:
E-mail:	
Birthday:	
Notes:	

G

Name:
Address:
Home: Cell:
Work: Fax:
E-mail:
Birthday:
Notes:

Name:
Address:
Home: Cell:
Work: Fax:
E-mail:
Birthday:
Notes:

Name:
Address:
Home: Cell:
Work: Fax:
E-mail:
Birthday:
Notes:

G

Name:	
Address:	
Home:	Cell:
Work:	Fax:
E-mail:	
Birthday:	
Notes:	

Name:	
Address:	
Home:	Cell:
Work:	Fax:
E-mail:	
Birthday:	
Notes:	

Name:	
Address:	
Home:	Cell:
Work:	Fax:
E-mail:	
Birthday:	
Notes:	

G

Name:	
Address:	
Home:	Cell:
Work:	Fax:
E-mail:	
Birthday:	
Notes:	

Name:	
Address:	
Home:	Cell:
Work:	Fax:
E-mail:	
Birthday:	
Notes:	

Name:	
Address:	
Home:	Cell:
Work:	Fax:
E-mail:	
Birthday:	
Notes:	

Name:
Address:

Home: Cell:
Work: Fax:
E-mail:
Birthday:
Notes:

Name:
Address:

Home: Cell:
Work: Fax:
E-mail:
Birthday:
Notes:

Name:
Address:

Home: Cell:
Work: Fax:
E-mail:
Birthday:
Notes:

H

Name:
Address:
Home:	Cell:
Work:	Fax:
E-mail:
Birthday:
Notes:

Name:
Address:
Home:	Cell:
Work:	Fax:
E-mail:
Birthday:
Notes:

Name:
Address:
Home:	Cell:
Work:	Fax:
E-mail:
Birthday:
Notes:

H

Name:	
Address:	
Home:	Cell:
Work:	Fax:
E-mail:	
Birthday:	
Notes:	

Name:	
Address:	
Home:	Cell:
Work:	Fax:
E-mail:	
Birthday:	
Notes:	

Name:	
Address:	
Home:	Cell:
Work:	Fax:
E-mail:	
Birthday:	
Notes:	

H

Name:	
Address:	
Home:	Cell:
Work:	Fax:
E-mail:	
Birthday:	
Notes:	

Name:	
Address:	
Home:	Cell:
Work:	Fax:
E-mail:	
Birthday:	
Notes:	

Name:	
Address:	
Home:	Cell:
Work:	Fax:
E-mail:	
Birthday:	
Notes:	

Name:
Address:

Home: Cell:
Work: Fax:
E-mail:
Birthday:
Notes:

Name:
Address:

Home: Cell:
Work: Fax:
E-mail:
Birthday:
Notes:

Name:
Address:

Home: Cell:
Work: Fax:
E-mail:
Birthday:
Notes:

Name:	
Address:	
Home:	Cell:
Work:	Fax:
E-mail:	
Birthday:	
Notes:	

Name:	
Address:	
Home:	Cell:
Work:	Fax:
E-mail:	
Birthday:	
Notes:	

Name:	
Address:	
Home:	Cell:
Work:	Fax:
E-mail:	
Birthday:	
Notes:	

Name:
Address:

Home: Cell:
Work: Fax:
E-mail:
Birthday:
Notes:

Name:
Address:

Home: Cell:
Work: Fax:
E-mail:
Birthday:
Notes:

Name:
Address:

Home: Cell:
Work: Fax:
E-mail:
Birthday:
Notes:

Name:	
Address:	
Home:	Cell:
Work:	Fax:
E-mail:	
Birthday:	
Notes:	

Name:	
Address:	
Home:	Cell:
Work:	Fax:
E-mail:	
Birthday:	
Notes:	

Name:	
Address:	
Home:	Cell:
Work:	Fax:
E-mail:	
Birthday:	
Notes:	

Name:

Address:

Home: | Cell:

Work: | Fax:

E-mail:

Birthday:

Notes:

Name:

Address:

Home: | Cell:

Work: | Fax:

E-mail:

Birthday:

Notes:

Name:

Address:

Home: | Cell:

Work: | Fax:

E-mail:

Birthday:

Notes:

J

Name:	
Address:	
Home:	Cell:
Work:	Fax:
E-mail:	
Birthday:	
Notes:	

Name:	
Address:	
Home:	Cell:
Work:	Fax:
E-mail:	
Birthday:	
Notes:	

Name:	
Address:	
Home:	Cell:
Work:	Fax:
E-mail:	
Birthday:	
Notes:	

J

Name:

Address:

Home:	Cell:
Work:	Fax:

E-mail:

Birthday:

Notes:

Name:

Address:

Home:	Cell:
Work:	Fax:

E-mail:

Birthday:

Notes:

Name:

Address:

Home:	Cell:
Work:	Fax:

E-mail:

Birthday:

Notes:

J

Name:	
Address:	
Home:	Cell:
Work:	Fax:
E-mail:	
Birthday:	
Notes:	

Name:	
Address:	
Home:	Cell:
Work:	Fax:
E-mail:	
Birthday:	
Notes:	

Name:	
Address:	
Home:	Cell:
Work:	Fax:
E-mail:	
Birthday:	
Notes:	

J

Name:
Address:
Home:	Cell:
Work:	Fax:
E-mail:
Birthday:
Notes:

Name:
Address:
Home:	Cell:
Work:	Fax:
E-mail:
Birthday:
Notes:

Name:
Address:
Home:	Cell:
Work:	Fax:
E-mail:
Birthday:
Notes:

K

Name:
Address:
Home: Cell:
Work: Fax:
E-mail:
Birthday:
Notes:

Name:
Address:
Home: Cell:
Work: Fax:
E-mail:
Birthday:
Notes:

Name:
Address:
Home: Cell:
Work: Fax:
E-mail:
Birthday:
Notes:

K

Name:	
Address:	
Home:	Cell:
Work:	Fax:
E-mail:	
Birthday:	
Notes:	

Name:	
Address:	
Home:	Cell:
Work:	Fax:
E-mail:	
Birthday:	
Notes:	

Name:	
Address:	
Home:	Cell:
Work:	Fax:
E-mail:	
Birthday:	
Notes:	

K

Name:	
Address:	
Home:	Cell:
Work:	Fax:
E-mail:	
Birthday:	
Notes:	

Name:	
Address:	
Home:	Cell:
Work:	Fax:
E-mail:	
Birthday:	
Notes:	

Name:	
Address:	
Home:	Cell:
Work:	Fax:
E-mail:	
Birthday:	
Notes:	

K

Name:	
Address:	
Home:	Cell:
Work:	Fax:
E-mail:	
Birthday:	
Notes:	

Name:	
Address:	
Home:	Cell:
Work:	Fax:
E-mail:	
Birthday:	
Notes:	

Name:	
Address:	
Home:	Cell:
Work:	Fax:
E-mail:	
Birthday:	
Notes:	

L

Name:

Address:
Home: Cell:
Work: Fax:
E-mail:
Birthday:
Notes:

Name:

Address:
Home: Cell:
Work: Fax:
E-mail:
Birthday:
Notes:

Name:

Address:
Home: Cell:
Work: Fax:
E-mail:
Birthday:
Notes:

Name:	
Address:	
Home:	Cell:
Work:	Fax:
E-mail:	
Birthday:	
Notes:	

Name:	
Address:	
Home:	Cell:
Work:	Fax:
E-mail:	
Birthday:	
Notes:	

Name:	
Address:	
Home:	Cell:
Work:	Fax:
E-mail:	
Birthday:	
Notes:	

L

Name:

Address:

Home:	Cell:
Work:	Fax:

E-mail:

Birthday:

Notes:

Name:

Address:

Home:	Cell:
Work:	Fax:

E-mail:

Birthday:

Notes:

Name:

Address:

Home:	Cell:
Work:	Fax:

E-mail:

Birthday:

Notes:

L

Name:	
Address:	
Home:	Cell:
Work:	Fax:
E-mail:	
Birthday:	
Notes:	

Name:	
Address:	
Home:	Cell:
Work:	Fax:
E-mail:	
Birthday:	
Notes:	

Name:	
Address:	
Home:	Cell:
Work:	Fax:
E-mail:	
Birthday:	
Notes:	

M

Name:	
Address:	
Home:	Cell:
Work:	Fax:
E-mail:	
Birthday:	
Notes:	

Name:	
Address:	
Home:	Cell:
Work:	Fax:
E-mail:	
Birthday:	
Notes:	

Name:	
Address:	
Home:	Cell:
Work:	Fax:
E-mail:	
Birthday:	
Notes:	

M

Name:
Address:
Home: Cell:
Work: Fax:
E-mail:
Birthday:
Notes:

Name:
Address:
Home: Cell:
Work: Fax:
E-mail:
Birthday:
Notes:

Name:
Address:
Home: Cell:
Work: Fax:
E-mail:
Birthday:
Notes:

M

Name:
Address:
Home: Cell:
Work: Fax:
E-mail:
Birthday:
Notes:

Name:
Address:
Home: Cell:
Work: Fax:
E-mail:
Birthday:
Notes:

Name:
Address:
Home: Cell:
Work: Fax:
E-mail:
Birthday:
Notes:

Name:
Address:

Home: Cell:
Work: Fax:
E-mail:
Birthday:
Notes:

Name:
Address:

Home: Cell:
Work: Fax:
E-mail:
Birthday:
Notes:

Name:
Address:

Home: Cell:
Work: Fax:
E-mail:
Birthday:
Notes:

N

Name:	
Address:	
Home:	Cell:
Work:	Fax:
E-mail:	
Birthday:	
Notes:	

Name:	
Address:	
Home:	Cell:
Work:	Fax:
E-mail:	
Birthday:	
Notes:	

Name:	
Address:	
Home:	Cell:
Work:	Fax:
E-mail:	
Birthday:	
Notes:	

Name:
Address:

Home: Cell:
Work: Fax:
E-mail:
Birthday:
Notes:

Name:
Address:

Home: Cell:
Work: Fax:
E-mail:
Birthday:
Notes:

Name:
Address:

Home: Cell:
Work: Fax:
E-mail:
Birthday:
Notes:

N

Name:

Address:

Home:	Cell:
Work:	Fax:

E-mail:
Birthday:
Notes:

Name:

Address:

Home:	Cell:
Work:	Fax:

E-mail:
Birthday:
Notes:

Name:

Address:

Home:	Cell:
Work:	Fax:

E-mail:
Birthday:
Notes:

N

Name:	
Address:	
Home:	Cell:
Work:	Fax:
E-mail:	
Birthday:	
Notes:	

Name:	
Address:	
Home:	Cell:
Work:	Fax:
E-mail:	
Birthday:	
Notes:	

Name:	
Address:	
Home:	Cell:
Work:	Fax:
E-mail:	
Birthday:	
Notes:	

O

Name:

Address:

Home:	Cell:
Work:	Fax:

E-mail:

Birthday:

Notes:

Name:

Address:

Home:	Cell:
Work:	Fax:

E-mail:

Birthday:

Notes:

Name:

Address:

Home:	Cell:
Work:	Fax:

E-mail:

Birthday:

Notes:

O

Name:	
Address:	
Home:	Cell:
Work:	Fax:
E-mail:	
Birthday:	
Notes:	

Name:	
Address:	
Home:	Cell:
Work:	Fax:
E-mail:	
Birthday:	
Notes:	

Name:	
Address:	
Home:	Cell:
Work:	Fax:
E-mail:	
Birthday:	
Notes:	

O

Name:

Address:

Home:	Cell:
Work:	Fax:

E-mail:

Birthday:

Notes:

Name:

Address:

Home:	Cell:
Work:	Fax:

E-mail:

Birthday:

Notes:

Name:

Address:

Home:	Cell:
Work:	Fax:

E-mail:

Birthday:

Notes:

O

Name:	
Address:	
Home:	Cell:
Work:	Fax:
E-mail:	
Birthday:	
Notes:	

Name:	
Address:	
Home:	Cell:
Work:	Fax:
E-mail:	
Birthday:	
Notes:	

Name:	
Address:	
Home:	Cell:
Work:	Fax:
E-mail:	
Birthday:	
Notes:	

P

Name:

Address:

Home:	Cell:
Work:	Fax:

E-mail:
Birthday:
Notes:

Name:

Address:

Home:	Cell:
Work:	Fax:

E-mail:
Birthday:
Notes:

Name:

Address:

Home:	Cell:
Work:	Fax:

E-mail:
Birthday:
Notes:

Name:
Address:

Home: Cell:
Work: Fax:
E-mail:
Birthday:
Notes:

Name:
Address:

Home: Cell:
Work: Fax:
E-mail:
Birthday:
Notes:

Name:
Address:

Home: Cell:
Work: Fax:
E-mail:
Birthday:
Notes:

P

Name:	
Address:	
Home:	Cell:
Work:	Fax:
E-mail:	
Birthday:	
Notes:	

Name:	
Address:	
Home:	Cell:
Work:	Fax:
E-mail:	
Birthday:	
Notes:	

Name:	
Address:	
Home:	Cell:
Work:	Fax:
E-mail:	
Birthday:	
Notes:	

P

Name:
Address:

Home: Cell:
Work: Fax:
E-mail:
Birthday:
Notes:

Name:
Address:

Home: Cell:
Work: Fax:
E-mail:
Birthday:
Notes:

Name:
Address:

Home: Cell:
Work: Fax:
E-mail:
Birthday:
Notes:

Q

Name:	
Address:	
Home:	Cell:
Work:	Fax:
E-mail:	
Birthday:	
Notes:	

Name:	
Address:	
Home:	Cell:
Work:	Fax:
E-mail:	
Birthday:	
Notes:	

Name:	
Address:	
Home:	Cell:
Work:	Fax:
E-mail:	
Birthday:	
Notes:	

Q

Name:

Address:

Home:	Cell:
Work:	Fax:

E-mail:
Birthday:
Notes:

Name:

Address:

Home:	Cell:
Work:	Fax:

E-mail:
Birthday:
Notes:

Name:

Address:

Home:	Cell:
Work:	Fax:

E-mail:
Birthday:
Notes:

Q

Name:

Address:

Home:	Cell:
Work:	Fax:

E-mail:
Birthday:
Notes:

Name:

Address:

Home:	Cell:
Work:	Fax:

E-mail:
Birthday:
Notes:

Name:

Address:

Home:	Cell:
Work:	Fax:

E-mail:
Birthday:
Notes:

Q

Name:
Address:

Home: Cell:
Work: Fax:
E-mail:
Birthday:
Notes:

Name:
Address:

Home: Cell:
Work: Fax:
E-mail:
Birthday:
Notes:

Name:
Address:

Home: Cell:
Work: Fax:
E-mail:
Birthday:
Notes:

R

Name:
Address:
Home: Cell:
Work: Fax:
E-mail:
Birthday:
Notes:

Name:
Address:
Home: Cell:
Work: Fax:
E-mail:
Birthday:
Notes:

Name:
Address:
Home: Cell:
Work: Fax:
E-mail:
Birthday:
Notes:

Name:
Address:

Home: Cell:
Work: Fax:
E-mail:
Birthday:
Notes:

Name:
Address:

Home: Cell:
Work: Fax:
E-mail:
Birthday:
Notes:

Name:
Address:

Home: Cell:
Work: Fax:
E-mail:
Birthday:
Notes:

R

Name:

Address:

Home:	Cell:
Work:	Fax:

E-mail:

Birthday:

Notes:

Name:

Address:

Home:	Cell:
Work:	Fax:

E-mail:

Birthday:

Notes:

Name:

Address:

Home:	Cell:
Work:	Fax:

E-mail:

Birthday:

Notes:

R

Name:	
Address:	
Home:	Cell:
Work:	Fax:
E-mail:	
Birthday:	
Notes:	

Name:	
Address:	
Home:	Cell:
Work:	Fax:
E-mail:	
Birthday:	
Notes:	

Name:	
Address:	
Home:	Cell:
Work:	Fax:
E-mail:	
Birthday:	
Notes:	

S

Name:
Address:
Home: Cell:
Work: Fax:
E-mail:
Birthday:
Notes:

Name:
Address:
Home: Cell:
Work: Fax:
E-mail:
Birthday:
Notes:

Name:
Address:
Home: Cell:
Work: Fax:
E-mail:
Birthday:
Notes:

S

Name:
Address:

Home: Cell:
Work: Fax:
E-mail:
Birthday:
Notes:

Name:
Address:

Home: Cell:
Work: Fax:
E-mail:
Birthday:
Notes:

Name:
Address:

Home: Cell:
Work: Fax:
E-mail:
Birthday:
Notes:

S

Name:	
Address:	
Home:	Cell:
Work:	Fax:
E-mail:	
Birthday:	
Notes:	

Name:	
Address:	
Home:	Cell:
Work:	Fax:
E-mail:	
Birthday:	
Notes:	

Name:	
Address:	
Home:	Cell:
Work:	Fax:
E-mail:	
Birthday:	
Notes:	

Name:
Address:

Home: Cell:
Work: Fax:
E-mail:
Birthday:
Notes:

Name:
Address:

Home: Cell:
Work: Fax:
E-mail:
Birthday:
Notes:

Name:
Address:

Home: Cell:
Work: Fax:
E-mail:
Birthday:
Notes:

T

Name:	
Address:	
Home:	Cell:
Work:	Fax:
E-mail:	
Birthday:	
Notes:	

Name:	
Address:	
Home:	Cell:
Work:	Fax:
E-mail:	
Birthday:	
Notes:	

Name:	
Address:	
Home:	Cell:
Work:	Fax:
E-mail:	
Birthday:	
Notes:	

T

Name:
Address:

Home: Cell:
Work: Fax:
E-mail:
Birthday:
Notes:

Name:
Address:

Home: Cell:
Work: Fax:
E-mail:
Birthday:
Notes:

Name:
Address:

Home: Cell:
Work: Fax:
E-mail:
Birthday:
Notes:

T

Name:

Address:

Home:	Cell:
Work:	Fax:
E-mail:	
Birthday:	
Notes:	

Name:

Address:

Home:	Cell:
Work:	Fax:
E-mail:	
Birthday:	
Notes:	

Name:

Address:

Home:	Cell:
Work:	Fax:
E-mail:	
Birthday:	
Notes:	

T

Name:	
Address:	
Home:	Cell:
Work:	Fax:
E-mail:	
Birthday:	
Notes:	

Name:	
Address:	
Home:	Cell:
Work:	Fax:
E-mail:	
Birthday:	
Notes:	

Name:	
Address:	
Home:	Cell:
Work:	Fax:
E-mail:	
Birthday:	
Notes:	

U

Name:	
Address:	
Home:	Cell:
Work:	Fax:
E-mail:	
Birthday:	
Notes:	

Name:	
Address:	
Home:	Cell:
Work:	Fax:
E-mail:	
Birthday:	
Notes:	

Name:	
Address:	
Home:	Cell:
Work:	Fax:
E-mail:	
Birthday:	
Notes:	

Name:
Address:

Home: Cell:
Work: Fax:
E-mail:
Birthday:
Notes:

Name:
Address:

Home: Cell:
Work: Fax:
E-mail:
Birthday:
Notes:

Name:
Address:

Home: Cell:
Work: Fax:
E-mail:
Birthday:
Notes:

U

Name:
Address:

Home: Cell:
Work: Fax:
E-mail:
Birthday:
Notes:

Name:
Address:

Home: Cell:
Work: Fax:
E-mail:
Birthday:
Notes:

Name:
Address:

Home: Cell:
Work: Fax:
E-mail:
Birthday:
Notes:

U

Name:
Address:

Home: Cell:
Work: Fax:
E-mail:
Birthday:
Notes:

Name:
Address:

Home: Cell:
Work: Fax:
E-mail:
Birthday:
Notes:

Name:
Address:

Home: Cell:
Work: Fax:
E-mail:
Birthday:
Notes:

V

Name:	
Address:	
Home:	Cell:
Work:	Fax:
E-mail:	
Birthday:	
Notes:	

Name:	
Address:	
Home:	Cell:
Work:	Fax:
E-mail:	
Birthday:	
Notes:	

Name:	
Address:	
Home:	Cell:
Work:	Fax:
E-mail:	
Birthday:	
Notes:	

V

Name:
Address:

Home: Cell:
Work: Fax:
E-mail:
Birthday:
Notes:

Name:
Address:

Home: Cell:
Work: Fax:
E-mail:
Birthday:
Notes:

Name:
Address:

Home: Cell:
Work: Fax:
E-mail:
Birthday:
Notes:

V

Name:
Address:

Home: Cell:
Work: Fax:
E-mail:
Birthday:
Notes:

Name:
Address:

Home: Cell:
Work: Fax:
E-mail:
Birthday:
Notes:

Name:
Address:

Home: Cell:
Work: Fax:
E-mail:
Birthday:
Notes:

V

Name:
Address:

Home:					Cell:
Work:					Fax:
E-mail:
Birthday:
Notes:

Name:
Address:

Home:					Cell:
Work:					Fax:
E-mail:
Birthday:
Notes:

Name:
Address:

Home:					Cell:
Work:					Fax:
E-mail:
Birthday:
Notes:

Name:

Address:

Home: Cell:

Work: Fax:

E-mail:

Birthday:

Notes:

Name:

Address:

Home: Cell:

Work: Fax:

E-mail:

Birthday:

Notes:

Name:

Address:

Home: Cell:

Work: Fax:

E-mail:

Birthday:

Notes:

Name:
Address:

Home: Cell:
Work: Fax:
E-mail:
Birthday:
Notes:

Name:
Address:

Home: Cell:
Work: Fax:
E-mail:
Birthday:
Notes:

Name:
Address:

Home: Cell:
Work: Fax:
E-mail:
Birthday:
Notes:

Name:	
Address:	
Home:	Cell:
Work:	Fax:
E-mail:	
Birthday:	
Notes:	

Name:	
Address:	
Home:	Cell:
Work:	Fax:
E-mail:	
Birthday:	
Notes:	

Name:	
Address:	
Home:	Cell:
Work:	Fax:
E-mail:	
Birthday:	
Notes:	

Name:
Address:

Home: Cell:
Work: Fax:
E-mail:
Birthday:
Notes:

Name:
Address:

Home: Cell:
Work: Fax:
E-mail:
Birthday:
Notes:

Name:
Address:

Home: Cell:
Work: Fax:
E-mail:
Birthday:
Notes:

Name:	
Address:	
Home:	Cell:
Work:	Fax:
E-mail:	
Birthday:	
Notes:	

Name:	
Address:	
Home:	Cell:
Work:	Fax:
E-mail:	
Birthday:	
Notes:	

Name:	
Address:	
Home:	Cell:
Work:	Fax:
E-mail:	
Birthday:	
Notes:	

Name:
Address:

Home: Cell:
Work: Fax:
E-mail:
Birthday:
Notes:

Name:
Address:

Home: Cell:
Work: Fax:
E-mail:
Birthday:
Notes:

Name:
Address:

Home: Cell:
Work: Fax:
E-mail:
Birthday:
Notes:

X

Name:
Address:

Home: | Cell:
Work: | Fax:
E-mail:
Birthday:
Notes:

Name:
Address:

Home: | Cell:
Work: | Fax:
E-mail:
Birthday:
Notes:

Name:
Address:

Home: | Cell:
Work: | Fax:
E-mail:
Birthday:
Notes:

X

Name:	
Address:	
Home:	Cell:
Work:	Fax:
E-mail:	
Birthday:	
Notes:	

Name:	
Address:	
Home:	Cell:
Work:	Fax:
E-mail:	
Birthday:	
Notes:	

Name:	
Address:	
Home:	Cell:
Work:	Fax:
E-mail:	
Birthday:	
Notes:	

Y

Name:	
Address:	
Home:	Cell:
Work:	Fax:
E-mail:	
Birthday:	
Notes:	

Name:	
Address:	
Home:	Cell:
Work:	Fax:
E-mail:	
Birthday:	
Notes:	

Name:	
Address:	
Home:	Cell:
Work:	Fax:
E-mail:	
Birthday:	
Notes:	

Name:
Address:

Home: Cell:
Work: Fax:
E-mail:
Birthday:
Notes:

Name:
Address:

Home: Cell:
Work: Fax:
E-mail:
Birthday:
Notes:

Name:
Address:

Home: Cell:
Work: Fax:
E-mail:
Birthday:
Notes:

Y

Name:
Address:
Home:	Cell:
Work:	Fax:
E-mail:
Birthday:
Notes:

Name:
Address:
Home:	Cell:
Work:	Fax:
E-mail:
Birthday:
Notes:

Name:
Address:
Home:	Cell:
Work:	Fax:
E-mail:
Birthday:
Notes:

Y

Name:
Address:

Home: Cell:
Work: Fax:
E-mail:
Birthday:
Notes:

Name:
Address:

Home: Cell:
Work: Fax:
E-mail:
Birthday:
Notes:

Name:
Address:

Home: Cell:
Work: Fax:
E-mail:
Birthday:
Notes:

Z

Name:

Address:

Home: | Cell:

Work: | Fax:

E-mail:

Birthday:

Notes:

Name:

Address:

Home: | Cell:

Work: | Fax:

E-mail:

Birthday:

Notes:

Name:

Address:

Home: | Cell:

Work: | Fax:

E-mail:

Birthday:

Notes:

Name:
Address:

Home: Cell:
Work: Fax:
E-mail:
Birthday:
Notes:

Name:
Address:

Home: Cell:
Work: Fax:
E-mail:
Birthday:
Notes:

Name:
Address:

Home: Cell:
Work: Fax:
E-mail:
Birthday:
Notes:

Z

Name:	
Address:	
Home:	Cell:
Work:	Fax:
E-mail:	
Birthday:	
Notes:	

Name:	
Address:	
Home:	Cell:
Work:	Fax:
E-mail:	
Birthday:	
Notes:	

Name:	
Address:	
Home:	Cell:
Work:	Fax:
E-mail:	
Birthday:	
Notes:	

Z

Name:
Address:

Home: Cell:
Work: Fax:
E-mail:
Birthday:
Notes:

Name:
Address:

Home: Cell:
Work: Fax:
E-mail:
Birthday:
Notes:

Name:
Address:

Home: Cell:
Work: Fax:
E-mail:
Birthday:
Notes:

Website Logins

WEBSITE: _____

USERNAME: _____

PASSWORD: _____

NOTES: _____

_____

_____

WEBSITE: _____

USERNAME: _____

PASSWORD: _____

NOTES: _____

_____

_____

WEBSITE: _____

USERNAME: _____

PASSWORD: _____

NOTES: _____

_____

_____

WEBSITE: _____

USERNAME: _____

PASSWORD: _____

NOTES: _____

_____

_____

Website Logins

WEBSITE: _____
USERNAME: _____
PASSWORD: _____
NOTES: _____
_____
_____

WEBSITE: _____
USERNAME: _____
PASSWORD: _____
NOTES: _____
_____
_____

WEBSITE: _____
USERNAME: _____
PASSWORD: _____
NOTES: _____
_____
_____

WEBSITE: _____
USERNAME: _____
PASSWORD: _____
NOTES: _____
_____
_____

Website Logins

WEBSITE: _____

USERNAME: _____

PASSWORD: _____

NOTES: _____

_____

_____

WEBSITE: _____

USERNAME: _____

PASSWORD: _____

NOTES: _____

_____

_____

WEBSITE: _____

USERNAME: _____

PASSWORD: _____

NOTES: _____

_____

_____

WEBSITE: _____

USERNAME: _____

PASSWORD: _____

NOTES: _____

_____

_____

Website Logins

WEBSITE: _____
USERNAME: _____
PASSWORD: _____
NOTES: _____

_____
_____

WEBSITE: _____
USERNAME: _____
PASSWORD: _____
NOTES: _____

_____
_____

WEBSITE: _____
USERNAME: _____
PASSWORD: _____
NOTES: _____

_____
_____

WEBSITE: _____
USERNAME: _____
PASSWORD: _____
NOTES: _____

_____
_____

Website Logins

WEBSITE: _____

USERNAME: _____

PASSWORD: _____

NOTES: _____

_____

_____

WEBSITE: _____

USERNAME: _____

PASSWORD: _____

NOTES: _____

_____

_____

WEBSITE: _____

USERNAME: _____

PASSWORD: _____

NOTES: _____

_____

_____

WEBSITE: _____

USERNAME: _____

PASSWORD: _____

NOTES: _____

_____

_____

Website Logins

WEBSITE: _____
USERNAME: _____
PASSWORD: _____
NOTES: _____
_____
_____

WEBSITE: _____
USERNAME: _____
PASSWORD: _____
NOTES: _____
_____
_____

WEBSITE: _____
USERNAME: _____
PASSWORD: _____
NOTES: _____
_____
_____

WEBSITE: _____
USERNAME: _____
PASSWORD: _____
NOTES: _____
_____
_____

Website Logins

WEBSITE: _____

USERNAME: _____

PASSWORD: _____

NOTES: _____

_____

_____

WEBSITE: _____

USERNAME: _____

PASSWORD: _____

NOTES: _____

_____

_____

WEBSITE: _____

USERNAME: _____

PASSWORD: _____

NOTES: _____

_____

_____

WEBSITE: _____

USERNAME: _____

PASSWORD: _____

NOTES: _____

_____

_____

Website Logins

WEBSITE: _____
USERNAME: _____
PASSWORD: _____
NOTES: _____
_____
_____
_____

WEBSITE: _____
USERNAME: _____
PASSWORD: _____
NOTES: _____
_____
_____
_____

WEBSITE: _____
USERNAME: _____
PASSWORD: _____
NOTES: _____
_____
_____
_____

WEBSITE: _____
USERNAME: _____
PASSWORD: _____
NOTES: _____
_____
_____
_____

Website Logins

WEBSITE: _____
USERNAME: _____
PASSWORD: _____
NOTES: _____
_____
_____

WEBSITE: _____
USERNAME: _____
PASSWORD: _____
NOTES: _____
_____
_____

WEBSITE: _____
USERNAME: _____
PASSWORD: _____
NOTES: _____
_____
_____

WEBSITE: _____
USERNAME: _____
PASSWORD: _____
NOTES: _____
_____
_____

Website Logins

WEBSITE: _____

USERNAME: _____

PASSWORD: _____

NOTES: _____

_____

_____

WEBSITE: _____

USERNAME: _____

PASSWORD: _____

NOTES: _____

_____

_____

WEBSITE: _____

USERNAME: _____

PASSWORD: _____

NOTES: _____

_____

_____

WEBSITE: _____

USERNAME: _____

PASSWORD: _____

NOTES: _____

_____

_____

Website Logins

WEBSITE: _____

USERNAME: _____

PASSWORD: _____

NOTES: _____

_____

_____

WEBSITE: _____

USERNAME: _____

PASSWORD: _____

NOTES: _____

_____

_____

WEBSITE: _____

USERNAME: _____

PASSWORD: _____

NOTES: _____

_____

_____

WEBSITE: _____

USERNAME: _____

PASSWORD: _____

NOTES: _____

_____

_____

Website Logins

WEBSITE: _____

USERNAME: _____

PASSWORD: _____

NOTES: _____

_____

_____

WEBSITE: _____

USERNAME: _____

PASSWORD: _____

NOTES: _____

_____

_____

WEBSITE: _____

USERNAME: _____

PASSWORD: _____

NOTES: _____

_____

_____

WEBSITE: _____

USERNAME: _____

PASSWORD: _____

NOTES: _____

_____

_____

Website Logins

WEBSITE: _____

USERNAME: _____

PASSWORD: _____

NOTES: _____

_____

_____

WEBSITE: _____

USERNAME: _____

PASSWORD: _____

NOTES: _____

_____

_____

WEBSITE: _____

USERNAME: _____

PASSWORD: _____

NOTES: _____

_____

_____

WEBSITE: _____

USERNAME: _____

PASSWORD: _____

NOTES: _____

_____

_____

Website Logins

WEBSITE: _____

USERNAME: _____

PASSWORD: _____

NOTES: _____

_____

_____

WEBSITE: _____

USERNAME: _____

PASSWORD: _____

NOTES: _____

_____

_____

WEBSITE: _____

USERNAME: _____

PASSWORD: _____

NOTES: _____

_____

_____

WEBSITE: _____

USERNAME: _____

PASSWORD: _____

NOTES: _____

_____

_____

Website Logins

WEBSITE: _____

USERNAME: _____

PASSWORD: _____

NOTES: _____

_____

_____

WEBSITE: _____

USERNAME: _____

PASSWORD: _____

NOTES: _____

_____

_____

WEBSITE: _____

USERNAME: _____

PASSWORD: _____

NOTES: _____

_____

_____

WEBSITE: _____

USERNAME: _____

PASSWORD: _____

NOTES: _____

_____

_____

Website Logins

WEBSITE: _____

USERNAME: _____

PASSWORD: _____

NOTES: _____

_____

_____

WEBSITE: _____

USERNAME: _____

PASSWORD: _____

NOTES: _____

_____

_____

WEBSITE: _____

USERNAME: _____

PASSWORD: _____

NOTES: _____

_____

_____

WEBSITE: _____

USERNAME: _____

PASSWORD: _____

NOTES: _____

_____

_____

Website Logins

WEBSITE: _____
USERNAME: _____
PASSWORD: _____
NOTES: _____
_____
_____

WEBSITE: _____
USERNAME: _____
PASSWORD: _____
NOTES: _____
_____
_____

WEBSITE: _____
USERNAME: _____
PASSWORD: _____
NOTES: _____
_____
_____

WEBSITE: _____
USERNAME: _____
PASSWORD: _____
NOTES: _____
_____
_____

Website Logins

WEBSITE: _____
USERNAME: _____
PASSWORD: _____
NOTES: _____
_____
_____

WEBSITE: _____
USERNAME: _____
PASSWORD: _____
NOTES: _____
_____
_____

WEBSITE: _____
USERNAME: _____
PASSWORD: _____
NOTES: _____
_____
_____

WEBSITE: _____
USERNAME: _____
PASSWORD: _____
NOTES: _____
_____
_____

Website Logins

WEBSITE: _____

USERNAME: _____

PASSWORD: _____

NOTES: _____

_____

_____

WEBSITE: _____

USERNAME: _____

PASSWORD: _____

NOTES: _____

_____

_____

WEBSITE: _____

USERNAME: _____

PASSWORD: _____

NOTES: _____

_____

_____

WEBSITE: _____

USERNAME: _____

PASSWORD: _____

NOTES: _____

_____

_____

Website Logins

WEBSITE: _____
USERNAME: _____
PASSWORD: _____
NOTES: _____
_____
_____

WEBSITE: _____
USERNAME: _____
PASSWORD: _____
NOTES: _____
_____
_____

WEBSITE: _____
USERNAME: _____
PASSWORD: _____
NOTES: _____
_____
_____

WEBSITE: _____
USERNAME: _____
PASSWORD: _____
NOTES: _____
_____
_____

Notes

Notes

Notes

Notes

Notes

Notes

Notes

Notes

Notes

Notes

Notes

Notes

Notes

Notes

Notes

Notes

Notes

Notes

Notes

Notes

Notes

Made in the USA
Middletown, DE
22 October 2023

41264298R00084